An Imprint of Desideramus Publish

First Edition

Published just after Joe Biden's Inauguration, 2021

Houston, Texas

We gotta do something!

ISBN: 978-0-9975883-9-2

For permission, or for information about custom editions, special sales and premium or corporate purchases, please contact Desideramus Publishing.

Beneficial Accomplishments of Joe Biden

By BB Denson

Contents

Introduction

Joe Biden has been a fixture of American Politics for going on 100 years.

We have seen him on CNN (Chinese News Network) and heard fabulous things about him from the renowned New York Lies.

As talented as he is, he could have been a wealthy man today, but instead devoted his life to public service.

He has done so much to make this country what it is today that we have him in large part to thank for the current state of our country. He has done as much or more than any of his Demoncrat colleagues. So many things in fact, that his inauguration seemed the perfect time to create this comprehensive guide to all of his beneficial accomplishments.

1.   Reduced **Healthcare** Costs

1.   Joe Biden and ObamaCare certainly did help lower Healthcare costs...

for members of Congress and their families.

~ 7 ~

~ 9 ~

~ 11 ~

2.   Advancement of Education

The United States has put more money into Education than any other country. In theory, it should be the envy of all other nations. Is it?

Here is a listing of the things Joe Biden did to contribute:

3.   Improved **Race Relations**

This country was founded on the principal of everyone being created equal. (Go check the Declaration of Independence.) The thing that divides a country is when one race is preferred or given special treatment over another. It is important to have a level playing field, whether it is with regard to hiring, getting into colleges, getting funding for education, treatment by law enforcement, or even a business earning a government contract. Otherwise racial tension ensues.

Here is a listing of all the things Joe Biden has done to ensure no preferential treatment for anyone of any race, creed, sex or color:

4.   Encouraged Free Speech

Communication, in particular social media, is growing at exponential speed. It is important that a variety of opinions and voices be heard. When only the opinions and viewpoints of one party are heard, countries inevitably become one party Communist States.

Here are the ways Joe Biden has worked with High Tech to encourage free speech:

5. **Safer** Cities

The Summer of 2020 saw massive amounts of rioting and looting in the largest cities of the United States. Buildings were torched, statues were toppled and people were killed.

Here are the things Joe Biden and the Demoncrats did to encourage peace in our cities:

6.   Strengthened the US Military:

Obviously it is important to fund the military, but it is also important that the military knows that their country is behind them. It is important that our veterans know we will take care of them after they have completed their service.

Here are the ways Joe helped strengthen the US Military, making it the most effective in history:

7.   Protected American **Intellectual Property** from China

I am thinking this was perhaps not a priority for Joe.

We are talking about China after all.

8.   Brought **Manufacturing Jobs**
Back to the USA

Oops, perhaps I was thinking of a different administration

with regard to this one.

9.   **United** the Country

When your party is in power, it is important that you reach across the aisle to work with the other side, to make sure that everyone's voice is being heard.

The fact that this section is blank is one of the saddest aspects of this book.

It is the one thing that Nancy and Joe could have done that would have changed everything else.

~ 93 ~

10. Made the USA a More
Prosperous Country

1.) Hunter Biden sure made a lot of money.

Does that count?

2.) Made the USA Energy Independent.

Darn it, once again, that was someone else!

11.   Ensured Free and
Fair Elections

Again, I got nothing.

If only they had audited the Dominion machines, it sure would have quelled a lot of the concern.

12. Made **Americans Proud** of the **USA** Again

Wouldn't it be nice to have something to list here?

CPSIA information can be obtained
at www.ICGtesting.com
Printed in the USA
FSHW021511100321
79263FS